CNN Short News

Vol. 1

Asahi Press

《《《 音声ストリーミング配信 》》》

http://text.asahipress.com/free/english/

この教科書の音声は、
上記ウェブサイトにて無料で配信しています。

CNN Short News, Vol. 1
Copyright © 2019 by Asahi Press

All rights reserved. No part of this book may be reproduced or transmitted in any form or by any means, electronic or mechanical, including photocopying, recording or by any information storage and retrieval system, without permission in writing from the authors and the publisher.

はしがき

　本書は、世界最大のニュース専門テレビ局CNNで放送されたニュースを基に編集された月刊英語学習誌『CNN English Express』の記事・音声から、短い英語ニュースを厳選して再編集された『CNNニュース・リスニング』に収録されたものを、英語授業の教材として活用できるようにしたものです。

　本書の音声は、『CNNニュース・リスニング』のCDに収録されていたCNN放送で使用された「ナチュラル音声」のほか、ナレーターがゆっくり読み直した音声が「ポーズ（無音の間）なし」と「ポーズあり」の3種類で収録されています。1教材あたり30秒程度なので、少なくとも3種類の音声を3回ずつ繰り返し聴くことによって、英語が自然に聞き取れるようになります。

　聴解能力にはしっかりとした語彙力が必要です。リスニングの前に語彙の確認と語彙の派生語を確認することによって語彙を増強しておくことも必要です。そして、リスニングでは前記の音声活用法をお勧めします。正確に聞き取れたかどうかを確認するために空所補充を行います。基本的なものばかりですので、基礎力の確認となります。次にニュースの内容に関して、全体的な主題、詳細事項の真偽、そしてTOEIC®テストPart 4形式による問題により演習に取り組みます。最後に、ニュースに出てきた表現を用いた整序問題形式の英作文を行います。

本書の構成は次のようになっています。
　・**DEFINITIONS**: 語彙の確認
　・**CHANGING WORDS**: 語彙の増強
　・**LISTENING**: 3つの種類の音声で聴解能力の増強
　・**WHAT'S IT ABOUT?**: ニュース内容の確認（主題）
　・**TRUE OR FALSE?**: ニュース内容の確認（詳細事項）
　・**TOEIC-STYLE QUESTIONS**: ニュース内容の確認（TOEIC®テストPart 4形式）
　・**EXPRESSIONS**: 表現能力の確認・増強

　本書は、主教材としても、副教材としても、あるいは、総合教材としても、リスニング教材としても、様々な活用の仕方ができるものです。また、学習者自身もそれぞれの工夫で学習に活用できるものとなっています。

　本書をきっかけに、月刊英語学習誌『CNN English Express』の購読、さらには、『CNNニュース・リスニング』を活用されて、生の英語に触れて、学習者の皆さんの英語聴解能力が向上するのを願っています。

　最後に、この度の企画を提案頂きました編集部の小川洋一郎氏、編集に際してご助言を頂きました加藤愛理氏に心からの感謝を申し上げます。

安浪誠祐
Richard S. Lavin

Unit 1 ▶ "SUPER-AGED" SOCIETIES 2

Unit 2 ▶ TOWARD LIVING ON THE MOON 6

Unit 3 ▶ DANGEROUS PROPOSAL 10

Unit 4 ▶ AUTOMATION THREATENS JOBS 14

Unit 5 ▶ HARVARD ACCUSED OF RACIAL BIAS 18

Unit 6 ▶ THOUGHT-CONTROLLED ARTIFICIAL ARMS 22

Unit 7 ▶ GUIDE TO MODERN MANNERS 26

Unit 8 ▶ ANCIENT CAVE ART IN INDONESIA 30

Unit 9 ▶ HEAT THREAT IN THE MIDDLE EAST 34

Unit 10 ▶ GROWING IMPACT OF PLASTIC ON SEABIRDS 38

Unit 11 ▶ CHINA'S LIFE-SHORTENING AIR 42

Unit 12 ▶ PROSTHETIC LIMBS FROM 3-D PRINTERS 46

Unit 13 ▶ NZ MAKES CYBERBULLYING ILLEGAL 50

Unit 14 ▶ MUSICAL TASTE AND PERSONALITY 54

Unit 15 ▶ MORNING-PERSON GENES 58

CNN Short News

Vol. 1

Asahi Press

UNIT 1
"SUPER-AGED" SOCIETIES

次の単語の定義として最も適当なものを選びなさい。

1) agency   (   )   (a) to divide into types
2) project   (   )   (b) to become older
3) categorize   (   )   (c) to increase
4) age   (   )   (d) a kind of organization
5) rise   (   )   (e) to predict

次の単語をカッコ内の形で答えなさい。

1) categorize [名詞] _____
2) society [形容詞] _____
3) rise [過去分詞] _____
4) rating [原形] _____
5) keep [過去分詞] _____

英語を聞いて、カッコ内を埋めなさい。

(_____) to the ratings agency Moody's, many countries are (_____) their populations aging faster than ever before. Moody's categorizes some societies as "super-aged": Italy, Germany and Japan. But it (_____) by 2020 there will be 13 and the number will (_____) rising. And it projects that in the next 15 years, only a handful of African countries will see a (_____) number of people of working age.

rating	格付け
population	(ある地域の) 全住民、人口
a handful of	一握りの
working age	生産年齢

本文の内容をまとめているものを選びなさい。

1) The populations of many countries are getting very old.
2) The reliability of ratings agencies is going down.
3) The developed world's problems are moving to Africa.

(　　)

本文の内容に合っていればTを、合っていなければFを書きなさい。

1) Many countries' populations are aging fast. ( )
2) Germany is the only "super-aged" society. ( )
3) Japan's population is getting younger. ( )

本文の内容に適合しているものを選びなさい。

1) In which countries will there be an increase in the working age population over the next 15 years?
   (a) Italy, Germany and Japan.
   (b) Some countries in Africa.
   (c) Some Asian countries. ( )

2) What is a super-aged society?
   (a) One in which more than one in five people is over 65 years of age.
   (b) One in which there are many aged people but the social security is excellent.
   (c) One in which there are many aged people but they live a good life.
   ( )

EXPRESSIONS

日本語の意味を表すように、本文中の単語を使って空所を埋めなさい。

1) 人口統計学者によると、日本の人口は 2010 年に減少し始めた。
   (   ) (   ) demographers, Japan's population began to decline in 2010.

2) アジアの開発途上国は、これまでよりも世界経済に影響を及ぼしている。
   Developing countries in Asia have more influence on the world economy (   ) (   ) (   ).

3) 1990 年代半ば以降に産まれた人たちは、ジェネレーション Z と分類されている。
   People born since the mid-1990s (   ) (   ) (   ) Generation Z.

4) 学期の終わりまでにすべての課題を提出する必要がある。
   You need to submit all your assignments (   ) (   ) (   ) (   ) the semester.

5) 新しいショッピングセンターが完成したあと、このあたりの道路は混雑が予想される。
   The roads around here are (   ) (   ) be congested after the new shopping center is completed.

UNIT 2
TOWARD LIVING ON THE MOON

DEFINITIONS

次の単語の定義として最も適当なものを選びなさい。

1) mankind （　　）
2) moon （　　）
3) habitable （　　）
4) probe （　　）
5) trace （　　）

(a) a small, unmanned spaceship used to take measurements
(b) the human race
(c) providing conditions that are suitable for living
(d) a sign that something was present or existed
(e) the earth's natural satellite

CHANGING WORDS

次の単語をカッコ内の形で答えなさい。

1) move ［名詞形］ _____
2) south ［形容詞形］ _____
3) pole ［形容詞形］ _____
4) replace ［名詞形］ _____
5) ISS ［3語で］ _____

UNIT 2

LISTENING

英語を聞いて、カッコ内を埋めなさい。

Now, Europe and Russia are hoping to move mankind one step (_____) to living on the moon. Space agencies from both [countries] are (_____) up to see if the moon is (_____) habitable for people. They're sending a probe to its south pole to find any traces of water, which could support life (_____) future missions. And there are even plans to send inflatable domes to the moon and (_____) a new lunar base to replace the International Space Station.

NOTES

> mission ………… [特定の目的を果たすための] 宇宙旅行、ミッション
> inflatable ……… 膨らませる、膨張式の
> lunar …………… 月面上の
> base …………… 基地
> replace ………… 〜を取り替える

WHAT'S IT ABOUT?

本文の内容をまとめているものを選びなさい。

1) Space agencies are working together to mine the moon for precious minerals.
2) Officials in Europe and Russia want to rebuild the International Space Station.
3) Scientists are looking into the possibility of living on the moon.

(   )

TRUE OR FALSE?

本文の内容に合っていればTを、合っていなければFを書きなさい。

1) Russia and Europe are working separately to investigate the moon. (   )
2) Scientists are sending a probe to the moon's north pole. (   )
3) Scientists are hoping to find water on the moon. (   )

TOEIC-STYLE QUESTIONS

本文の内容に適合しているものを選びなさい。

1) Why do space agencies want to send inflatable domes to the moon?
   (a) The domes could be used to protect the International Space Station.
   (b) The domes could be used to build a lunar base.
   (c) Scientists want to know whether the domes will work in low gravity.

   (   )

2) What do scientists hope to find at the moon's south pole?
   (a) The domes that they sent to the moon on earlier missions.
   (b) Evidence of life.
   (c) Water.   (   )

UNIT 2

日本語の意味を表すように、本文中の単語を使って空所を埋めなさい。

1) どうやってヒトが長期間にわたって宇宙で健康に生活できるかということを科学者は最終的に知りたいと考えている。
   Scientists (　　　　) eventually (　　　　) learn how humans can live healthily in space over the long term.

2) もし気分が良くないなら、日を改めて試験を受けることができるかどうか考えてみるべきだ。
   If you're feeling sick, you should (　　　　) (　　　　) it's possible to take the exam on another day.

3) 7世紀に、日本は進んだ技術や芸術やその他のことを学ぶために中国の王宮に特命使節を派遣した。
   In the 7th century, Japan (　　　　) envoys (　　　　) the Chinese court (　　　　) learn advanced technology, arts, and other matters.

4) ブラックホールによって発せられる力と同様のもの凄い重力が時空を曲げる可能性があり、これが理論的にタイムトラベルを可能にするだろう。
   Huge gravitational forces, similar to those emitted by black holes, can bend time, (　　　　) theoretically would make time travel possible.

5) 有名なレストランは、勤務時間中に従業員がボランティア活動をするのを許している。そして、この計画をより広く広めようというプランさえ持っている。
   A well-known restaurant allows some employees to do volunteer work during work hours, and there (　　　　) (　　　　) plans to expand the scheme much wider.

UNIT 3
DANGEROUS PROPOSAL

DEFINITIONS

次の単語の定義として最も適当なものを選びなさい。

1) crane　　（　　）
2) roof　　　（　　）
3) evacuate （　　）
4) stabilize （　　）
5) wedding （　　）

(a) the top, outer part of a building
(b) to leave a building for safety reasons
(c) to make something secure and unlikely to move
(d) a tall machine used to move heavy objects and work on buildings
(e) a ceremony in which two people get married

CHANGING WORDS

次の単語をカッコ内の形で答えなさい。

1) romantic [名詞形] _____
2) lend [反意語] _____
3) happy [名詞形] _____
4) hurt [過去形] _____
5) hope [形容詞形] _____

UNIT 3

LISTENING

英語を聞いて、カッコ内を埋めなさい。

What a Dutch man (_____) to be a romantic evening with his girlfriend—well, it turned into a "smashing proposal." He (_____) a crane with the hope of reaching his girlfriend's window to propose. (_____), the crane tipped over [and] crashed through the roof of the home next door. Whoops! Thirty-two homes were evacuated (_____) crews stabilized the crane. We're happy to say no one was (_____). And if you're wondering—she still said yes. Hope the wedding goes a little more smoothly.

NOTES

smashing ……… 素晴らしい
reach …………… [目的地に] 達する
tip ……………… 傾く

WHAT'S IT ABOUT?

本文の内容をまとめているものを選びなさい。

1) Cranes are unstable, dangerous machines.
2) A man's plan to propose to his girlfriend went wrong.
3) It is important to use one's imagination when proposing marriage.

(   )

本文の内容に合っていればTを、合っていなければFを書きなさい。

1) A Dutch man bought a crane. （　　）

2) The evening went as the Dutch man planned. （　　）

3) The crane fell over. （　　）

本文の内容に適合しているものを選びなさい。

1) Why did a Dutch man rent a crane?

   (a) He wanted to inspect the window of a friend's house.

   (b) He wanted to propose to his girlfriend through her window.

   (c) He needed practice for his job.

                                                            （　　）

2) What happened when the crane tipped over?

   (a) The Dutch man was injured.

   (b) It smashed the window of his girlfriend's house.

   (c) It crashed through the roof of a neighboring house.

                                                            （　　）

UNIT 3

日本語の意味を表すように、本文中の単語を使って空所を埋めなさい。

1) 映画監督は2013年の映画を最後のものにするつもりだったが、年齢にもかかわらず、復帰を果たす気持ちを抑えることができなかった。
The director (　　　　　) the 2013 film to be his final one, but, despite his age, couldn't resist making a comeback.

2) 責任をもって土地と水を管理すれば、乾燥地が砂漠に変わるのを防ぐことができる。
Managing land and water responsibly can prevent dry land (　　　　) (　　　　) desert.

3) 数百万の人が、どこの家庭でも通じる名前の俳優になる希望を抱いてハリウッドへ行く。
Millions of people move to Hollywood (　　　　) (　　　　) (　　　　) (　　　　) becoming household names.

4) あなたが試験を見事にパスしたことを知らせることができてうれしい。
I'm happy (　　　　) (　　　　) (　　　　) you passed the test with flying colors.

5) あなたの前には長旅がある。すべてが順調に行くといいですね。
You have a long trip in front of you. I hope everything (　　　　) (　　　　).

13

UNIT 4
AUTOMATION THREATENS JOBS

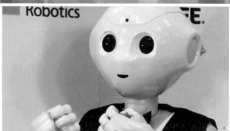

 DEFINITIONS

次の単語の定義として最も適当なものを選びなさい。

1) charity （　）
2) employment （　）
3) musician （　）
4) designer （　）
5) farmer （　）

(a) someone whose job is to decide how products will work or look
(b) someone who composes or performs music
(c) work, usually done to earn money
(d) a person who grows crops or raises animals
(e) an organization for helping people in need

 CHANGING WORDS

次の単語をカッコ内の形で答えなさい。

1) creative [名詞形] _____
2) innovation [動詞形] _____
3) archivist [動詞形] _____
4) employment [「従業員」英語で] _____
5) journalist [「ジャーナリズム」英語で] _____

UNIT 4

LISTENING

英語を聞いて、カッコ内を埋めなさい。

Well, (_____) a robot take over your job? If you're not creative (_____), you may be at risk. An innovation charity, Nesta, says the UK needs around 1 million new creative jobs by 2030 to keep humans in employment. Who's safe from robots? Artists, musicians, (_____) designers—and it turns out journalists are looking OK (_____). People who work (_____) archivists, farmers and accountants, however, are among those the group found to be under threat.

NOTES

NESTA ……… ネスタ、英国国立科学・技術・芸術基金
　　　　　　(National Endowment for Science, Technology and the Arts)
UK …………… イギリス (United Kingdom)
archivist ……… 文書保管人
accountant …… 会計士

WHAT'S IT ABOUT?

本文の内容をまとめているものを選びなさい。

1) People with non-creative jobs are at risk of being replaced by robots.
2) Nesta is researching the appropriate roles of robots in society.
3) The UK needs more robots to solve the problem of an aging population.

(　　　)

TRUE OR FALSE?

本文の内容に合っていればTを、合っていなければFを書きなさい。

1) In the UK, people with creative jobs are likely to lose them to robots. ( )

2) To maintain employment, the UK needs more creative jobs. ( )

3) Artists are not in much danger of losing their jobs to robots. ( )

TOEIC-STYLE QUESTIONS

本文の内容に適合しているものを選びなさい。

1) What kinds of jobs are considered safe from replacement by robots?
   (a) Archivists and artists.
   (b) Artists and musicians.
   (c) Farmers. ( )

2) What kinds of jobs are considered to be in danger of replacement?
   (a) Journalists, archivists, and accountants.
   (b) Artists, musicians, and graphic designers.
   (c) Archivists, farmers, and accountants. ( )

EXPRESSIONS

日本語の意味を表すように、本文中の単語を使って空所を埋めなさい。

1) 創立者が60歳に達したときに、彼の息子が毎日の会社運営を引き継いだ。

   When the founder reached the age of 60, his son (　　　　　) (　　　　　) the day-to-day running of the company.

2) ほとんどの蚊がウイルスを広めるわけではないが、刺された誰もがある程度の危険にさらされる。

   Although most mosquitoes don't spread viruses, everyone who has been bitten is (　　　　　) some (　　　　　).

3) なりすまし犯罪から安全でいられるためには、長くて推測するのが難しいパスワードを使う必要がある。

   In order to remain (　　　　　) (　　　　　) identity theft, it is necessary to use long and difficult-to-guess passwords.

4) 南アフリカでは、その土地を使っている人たちの間でそれを共有するキャンペーンがある。

   In South Africa, there is a campaign to share the land (　　　　　) (　　　　　) who work it.

5) チーターやトラやキリンはみな絶滅の脅威にさらされていると言われている。

   The cheetah, tiger, and giraffe are all said to be (　　　　　) (　　　　　) of extinction.

HARVARD ACCUSED OF RACIAL BIAS

DEFINITIONS

次の単語の定義として最も適当なものを選びなさい。

1) coalition　　（　　）　　(a) a temporary union of groups
2) file　　　　　（　　）　　(b) a prize or other honor
3) complaint　（　　）　　(c) to proudly tell people of your
4) boast　　　　（　　）　　　　achievements
5) accolade　　（　　）　　(d) a statement of dissatisfaction
　　　　　　　　　　　　　　　　(e) to take official action

CHANGING WORDS

次の単語をカッコ内の形で答えなさい。

1) discrimination ［動詞形］ _____
2) hold ［過去分詞形］ _____
3) applicant ［動詞形］ _____
4) standard ［動詞形］ _____
5) acceptance ［動詞形］ _____

英語を聞いて、カッコ内を埋めなさい。

Here's a question, now, (＿＿＿＿＿＿) Harvard University: Is the university trying to keep Asian Americans out? A coalition of more than 60 Asian American groups has filed a (＿＿＿＿＿＿) racial-discrimination complaint against the school. The coalition accuses Harvard of (＿＿＿＿＿＿) holding Asian American applicants to a higher standard. The complaint says Asian Americans have the lowest acceptance (＿＿＿＿＿＿) despite boasting some of the highest test (＿＿＿＿＿＿) and accolades.

NOTES

Harvard University …… ハーバード大学（米国最古の研究型私立大学で、アイビー・リーグの一校）
racial …………………… 人種の
unfairly ………………… 不当に
accolade ………………… 栄誉

 WHAT'S IT ABOUT?

本文の内容をまとめているものを選びなさい。

1) Asian Americans do not study hard enough.
2) 60% of Asian Americans are clever enough to go to Harvard University.
3) Some Asian Americans say that they are held to a higher standard than other groups by Harvard University.

(　　　)

TRUE OR FALSE?

本文の内容に合っていればTを、合っていなければFを書きなさい。

1) There is a suspicion that Harvard University is being unfair to Asian Americans. (　　)

2) Some Asian American groups have filed an official complaint. (　　)

3) Asian Americans generally have low test scores. (　　)

TOEIC-STYLE QUESTIONS

本文の内容に適合しているものを選びなさい。

1) What kind of complaint have some Asian-American groups filed?
   (a) A racial-discrimination complaint.
   (b) A complaint in support of federalism.
   (c) A request for unconditional acceptance. (　　)

2) How do Asian Americans' test scores compare to those of other racial groups?
   (a) They are lower than most.
   (b) They are higher than most.
   (c) They are about the same. (　　)

UNIT 5

EXPRESSIONS

日本語の意味を表すように、本文中の単語を使って空所を埋めなさい。

1) 庭から雑草を除去する良い方法の一つは、それらに酢を噴霧することだ。
   One good way to (　　　　) weeds (　　　　) of your garden is to spray vinegar on them.

2) 誰かが悪事を働くのを非難するとき、証拠を示すことが必要だ。
   When (　　　　) someone (　　　　) wrongdoing, it is necessary to present evidence.

3) 政治家は高い倫理基準に縛られる必要がある。
   Politicians need to be (　　　　) (　　　　) high ethical standards.

4) 何カ月も勉強したけれども、その学生は試験にぎりぎりのところで合格できなかった。
   (　　　　) (　　　　) for many months, the student narrowly failed to pass the exam.

5) 消費者を欺く会社に対して苦情を申し立てることは可能だ。
   It is possible to file (　　　　) (　　　　) companies that mislead consumers.

UNIT 6
THOUGHT-CONTROLLED ARTIFICIAL ARMS

DEFINITIONS

次の単語の定義として最も適当なものを選びなさい。

1) future　　　（　　）
2) limb　　　 （　　）
3) patient　　 （　　）
4) invention　 （　　）
5) technology （　　）

(a) the time that follows the present time
(b) scientific knowledge or the applications of that knowledge
(c) a leg or arm
(d) a machine or tool that has been thought of for the first time
(e) someone who is receiving medical treatment

CHANGING WORDS

次の単語をカッコ内の形で答えなさい。

1) create ［名詞形］ _____
2) artificial ［反意語］ _____
3) accident ［形容詞形］ _____
4) first ［反意語］ _____
5) incredible ［名詞形］ _____

UNIT 6

LISTENING

英語を聞いて、カッコ内を埋めなさい。

Thought-controlled robotic arms may sound like a (＿＿＿＿＿＿) of the future, but they have become (＿＿＿＿＿＿). Scientists at Johns Hopkins University created the artificial limbs. One man who (＿＿＿＿＿＿) his arms 40 years ago in an accident became the first patient to try out the new invention. And he can move these arms just by thinking about moving his arms. Researchers say this is just a (＿＿＿＿＿＿)—that the next 10 years will bring (＿＿＿＿＿＿) advances in the technology.

NOTES

thought-controlled ………… 脳波で動く、思考制御の
Johns Hopkins University … ジョンズ・ホプキンス大学
　　　　　　　　　　　　　（米国の特に医学分野で有名な私立の大学）
advance …………………… 進歩

WHAT'S IT ABOUT?

本文の内容をまとめているものを選びなさい。

1) Artificial limbs are now a reality.
2) Johns Hopkins University scientists are working hard on robotic arms and other technologies.
3) Many people lose their arms in accidents.　　　　　　　（　　）

TRUE OR FALSE?

本文の内容に合っていればTを、合っていなければFを書きなさい。

1) It is hoped that one day artificial limbs will become a reality. (　　)

2) Artificial arms were created by scientists at Johns Hopkins University. (　　)

3) Researchers think that advances in artificial limbs are unlikely. (　　)

TOEIC-STYLE QUESTIONS

本文の内容に適合しているものを選びなさい。

1) Who was the first person to try out artificial limbs created by Johns Hopkins University researchers?
   (a) A man who recently lost his limbs fighting in a war.
   (b) A woman working at Johns Hopkins.
   (c) A man who lost his arms in an accident. (　　)

2) How are the artificial arms moved?
   (a) The man operates them using a computer.
   (b) The man cannot move them himself.
   (c) The man just thinks about moving them. (　　)

UNIT 6

EXPRESSIONS

日本語の意味を表すように、本文中の単語を使って空所を埋めなさい。

1) あなたの休暇の計画はとても楽しそうだね。

   Your holiday plans (　　　　) (　　　　) a lot of fun!

2) 新しいパソコンを買ったよ。試しに使ってみてもいいよ。

   I've bought a new computer. Why don't you (　　　　) it (　　　　)?

3) もし本当に英語を上達したいなら、留学することを考えるべきだ。

   If you really want to improve your English, you should think (　　　　) (　　　　) abroad.

4) 次の数十年でロンドンやニューヨークやシドニーやその他の世界の主な都市が洪水に襲われるかもしれないと気象学者は言う。

   Climatologists say that the next few decades may (　　　　) flooding to London, New York, Sydney, and other major world cities.

5) 2030年までのコンピューティングの進歩として、病気を治療するために身体の中に入ることができるナノ・コンピュータがあると、コンピュータ科学者は予測する。

   Computer scientists predict that (　　　　) (　　　　) computing by 2030 will include nano-computers that can go inside the body to cure disease.

UNIT 7
GUIDE TO MODERN MANNERS

次の単語の定義として最も適当なものを選びなさい。

1) company　　（　　）
2) etiquette　　（　　）
3) update　　（　　）
4) guide　　（　　）
5) blind-copy　（　　）

(a) a book that gives instructions on a specific subject
(b) an organization that sells goods or services
(c) to send an email to someone without the other recipients' knowledge
(d) to add the latest information
(e) a set of guidelines for behavior

次の単語をカッコ内の形で答えなさい。

1) advise［名詞形］＿＿＿＿＿＿＿＿＿＿＿＿＿＿
2) public［反意語］＿＿＿＿＿＿＿＿＿＿＿＿＿＿
3) social［名詞形］＿＿＿＿＿＿＿＿＿＿＿＿＿＿
4) acceptable［名詞形］＿＿＿＿＿＿＿＿＿＿＿＿
5) consider［名詞形］＿＿＿＿＿＿＿＿＿＿＿＿＿

UNIT 7

英語を聞いて、カッコ内を埋めなさい。

Thanks to Debrett's, a company that has (_____) the British public on social etiquette for almost 250 years, we have an updated guide to modern (_____) in the 21st century for you. According to Debrett's, it's never acceptable to pay more attention to a phone (_____) the person in front of you. And if you're considering blind-copying someone (_____) an e-mail, Debrett's says this should be used with discretion, (_____) it may be deceptive.

almost ······· ほとんどの、もう少しで（近いがもう少しである状態に達していないこと）
deceptive ··· 人を誤解させるような

本文の内容をまとめているものを選びなさい。
1) British etiquette is very different from that in the U.S.
2) Debrett's guide can now be downloaded onto a phone.
3) A guide to manners has recently been updated.

(   )

TRUE OR FALSE?

本文の内容に合っていればTを、合っていなければFを書きなさい。

1) When you are busy, it is acceptable to concentrate on your phone more than on the person you are with. (   )
2) Blind-copying emails is a good general practice. (   )
3) Debrett's was founded in the 21st century. (   )

TOEIC-STYLE QUESTIONS

本文の内容に適合しているものを選びなさい。

1) In what area does Debrett's give advice?
    (a) In business strategy.
    (b) In social etiquette.
    (c) In email technologies. (   )

2) In what country is Debrett's based?
    (a) In the U.S.
    (b) In the U.K.
    (c) In Ireland. (   )

UNIT 7

日本語の意味を表すように、本文中の単語を使って空所を埋めなさい。

1) ある経済学者によると、数年以内に金融危機が再び起こりそうだ。

　　（　　　　　）（　　　　　　）some economists, another financial crisis is likely to occur in the next few years.

2) グリーン・レボリューション(農業技術の改良による穀物の増産)のおかげで、食糧の世界的な生産量が大幅に増加した。

　　（　　　　　）（　　　　　　）the Green Revolution, worldwide production of food has increased greatly.

3) どんなに忙しくても、自分自身の健康に注意をはらうのは大切だ。

　　However busy you are, it's important to (　　　　　)
　　（　　　　　）（　　　　　　） your own health.

4) 資産運用の専門家は、退職のために給与の約15％を貯えようと考えるべきであると言う。

　　Financial planners say that people should (　　　　　)
　　（　　　　　） around 15% of their salary for their retirement.

5) アメリカではあまりにも多くの子どもたちが薬を処方されていると懸念されていて、医師は慎重にADHDの薬を処方するように求められている。

　　Amidst worries that too many children in the U.S. are medicalized, doctors are being asked to prescribe ADHD drugs (　　　　　)
　　（　　　　　）.

29

UNIT 8
ANCIENT CAVE ART IN INDONESIA

次の単語の定義として最も適当なものを選びなさい。

1) amazing   (　　)   (a) a valuable discovery
2) find   (　　)   (b) a big hole in the ground
3) limestone   (　　)   (c) earlier; before
4) cave   (　　)   (d) very surprising
5) previously (　　)   (e) a kind of white or gray stone

次の単語をカッコ内の形で答えなさい。

1) archaeological [学問としての名詞形] _____
2) discover [名詞形] _____
3) island [人を表す名詞形] _____
4) European [名詞形] _____
5) examine [名詞形] _____

UNIT 8

LISTENING

英語を聞いて、カッコ内を埋めなさい。

(_____), from a very new sport to some very old art: an amazing archaeological find out of Indonesia. Researchers discovered hand (_____) in seven limestone caves on the island of Sulawesi. They could be as old as the (_____) European cave art, dating back 40,000 years. Sulawesi's cave art was (_____) thought to be only 10,000 years old. Archaeologists examined 12 images of human (_____) and two figures of animals in the cave.

NOTES

Indonesia ……… インドネシア（人口世界4番の国で、世界最大のムスリム人口を有する）
hand painting …… 手形の絵
Sulawesi ………… スラウェシ島（インドネシアのほぼ中央に位置している）

WHAT'S IT ABOUT?

本文の内容をまとめているものを選びなさい。

1) Many researchers have been visiting Indonesia in recent years.
2) There are more limestone caves in Indonesia than originally assumed.
3) Researchers have found hand paintings in Sulawesi that they think may be about 40,000 years old.

(　　)

TRUE OR FALSE?

本文の内容に合っていればTを、合っていなければFを書きなさい。

1) Researchers have found hand paintings in caves on an Indonesian island. (　　)

2) Sulawesi's cave art is 10,000 years old. (　　)

3) Archaeologists wonder why all the paintings are of human hands.
   (　　)

TOEIC-STYLE QUESTIONS

本文の内容に適合しているものを選びなさい。

1) What have researchers found in Indonesia?
   (a) A new island.
   (b) Some old cave art.
   (c) Evidence that humans originated in Asia. (　　)

2) How old is the cave art likely to be?
   (a) It was originally believed to be 40,000 years old, but now it is thought to be 10,000 years old.
   (b) It was originally believed to be 10,000 years old, but now it is thought to be 40,000 years old.
   (c) It is probably older than Europe. (　　)

UNIT 8

日本語の意味を表すように、本文中の単語を使って空所を埋めなさい。

1) ユヴァル・ノア・ハラリの書籍は、人工知能からマーク・ザッカーバーグまでの幅広い話題を取り上げる。

   Yuval Noah Harari's books cover a wide range of topics, (　　　　) artificial intelligence (　　　　) Mark Zuckerberg.

2) 大気中の二酸化炭素のレベルが、2050年までに550ppmの濃度までになることがあると環境保護論者は言う。

   Environmentalists say that CO_2 levels in the atmosphere could go (　　　　) high (　　　　) 550 parts per million by 2050.

3) ハロウィーンの起源は2000年以上前にさかのぼる。

   The origins of Halloween (　　　　)(　　　　) more than 2000 years.

4) ペンシルベニアのモラビア・ブック・ショップは世界で最も古い書店であると考えられている。

   The Moravian Book Shop in Pennsylvania (　　　　)(　　　　)(　　　　)(　　　　) the oldest bookshop in the world.

5) 数千人の男性のカルテを調べた研究者は、背の低い男性は心臓病に罹るリスクが高いことを発見した。

   Researchers (　　　　)(　　　　) the medical records of thousands of men found that short men had a greater risk of heart attack.

UNIT 9
HEAT THREAT IN THE MIDDLE EAST

DEFINITIONS

次の単語の定義として最も適当なものを選びなさい。

1) catastrophe (　　)　　(a) a disaster
2) gulf (　　)　　(b) a bay
3) extreme (　　)　　(c) accompanying
4) companion (　　)　　(d) to say that something is true
5) claim (　　)　　(e) very great

CHANGING WORDS

次の単語をカッコ内の形で答えなさい。

1) much [最上級] _____
2) global [名詞形] _____
3) prediction [動詞形] _____
4) survive [名詞形] _____
5) publish [名詞形] _____

34

LISTENING

英語を聞いて、カッコ内を埋めなさい。

Two degrees Celsius—it doesn't seem like much, but (＿＿＿＿＿) say if global average temperatures warm more than that, it could lead to climate catastrophe, like a frightening new prediction for parts of the Middle East, (＿＿＿＿＿) around the Persian Gulf. One day, it could be too hot for humans to survive in (＿＿＿＿＿) such as Doha, Dubai and Abu Dhabi. Now, the study, published in *Nature Climate Change*, says the extreme heat could hit within a (＿＿＿＿＿). A companion study claims air temperatures could (＿＿＿＿＿) as high as 60 degrees Celsius.

NOTES

Celsius	摂氏
frightening	恐ろしい
Doha	ドーハ（カタールの首都、カタール半島東海岸のペルシャ湾に面した港町）
Dubai	ドバイ（アラブ首長国連邦のひとつであるドバイ首長国の首都）
Abu Dhabi	アブダビ（アラブ首長国連邦のひとつであるアブダビ首長国の首都と連邦の首都を兼ねる）
Nature Climate Change	『ネイチャー・クライメート・チェンジ』誌

WHAT'S IT ABOUT?

本文の内容をまとめているものを選びなさい。

1) Doha and Dubai are the hottest cities on the planet.
2) It is possible that some parts of the Middle East will become too hot for humans to live.
3) *Nature Climate Change* has improved its analysis of weather trends.

(　　)

TRUE OR FALSE?

本文の内容に合っていればTを、合っていなければFを書きなさい。

1) Scientists are worried about a rise in temperature in the Persian Gulf. (　　)

2) Abu Dhabi is one of the cities where humans may no longer be able to live. (　　)

3) Temperatures up to sixty degrees Celsius are fine for humans to live. (　　)

TOEIC-STYLE QUESTIONS

本文の内容に適合しているものを選びなさい。

1) For which area of the world are scientists most worried about climate change?
   (a) Africa.
   (b) Europe as a whole.
   (c) The Middle East. (　　)

2) When do the scientists who wrote the article expect extreme heat to come?
   (a) Within the next decade.
   (b) Within a century.
   (c) Within a millennium. (　　)

UNIT 9

日本語の意味を表すように、本文中の単語を使って空所を埋めなさい。

1) 税率を引き下げると大統領は言ったが、それは良い考えのようには思えない。
   The president said he would decrease taxes, but that doesn't (　　　　)(　　　　) a good idea to me.

2) 食べすぎと運動不足は裕福病の原因となる可能性がある。
   Overeating and a lack of exercise can (　　　　)(　　　　) diseases of affluence.

3) あなたの持ち物は私には重すぎで車に運べない。運送会社を使う方が良い。
   Your belongings are too heavy (　　　　) me (　　　　) transport in my car. You'd better use a transportation company.

4) 今年の悪天候は、食品価格が倍になる可能性があるということを意味する。
   The bad weather this year means that food prices could (　　　　) much (　　　　) double.

5) 物理学の進歩は、いつかタイムトラベルが実現するかもしれないことを示唆する。
   Advances in physics suggest that (　　　　)(　　　　) time travel may become possible.

UNIT 10
GROWING IMPACT OF PLASTIC ON SEABIRDS

DEFINITIONS

次の単語の定義として最も適当なものを選びなさい。

1) environment (　　)
2) incredible (　　)
3) garbage (　　)
4) float (　　)
5) stomach (　　)

(a) very surprising, or difficult to believe
(b) the natural world
(c) rubbish, waste materials
(d) to rest or move slowly on the surface of a fluid
(e) a part of the body used to digest food

CHANGING WORDS

次の単語をカッコ内の形で答えなさい。

1) ocean ［形容詞形］ _____
2) nation ［形容詞形］ _____
3) academy ［形容詞形］ _____
4) science ［形容詞形］ _____
5) rise ［過去形］ _____

UNIT 10

LISTENING

英語を聞いて、カッコ内を埋めなさい。

We have one (_____) note on the environment and the incredible amount of garbage (_____) around the world's oceans and the impact that has on seabirds. A new study (_____) by the National Academy of Sciences says fewer than 10 percent of seabirds (_____) were studied during the 1970s and '80s were found to have plastic in their stomachs. That number—well, it's (_____) up to 90 percent. It's expected to rise to 99 percent by 2050.

NOTES

> incredible …… 信じられないほどの、途方もない
> amount ……… 量
> impact ……… 影響
> National Academy of Sciences …… 全米科学アカデミー
> up to ………… ～に至るまで、最高で～まで、～以下の

WHAT'S IT ABOUT?

本文の内容をまとめているものを選びなさい。

1) Garbage in the oceans is having a big impact on seabirds.
2) The amount of plastic in the oceans seems likely to grow.
3) The National Academy of Sciences has begun to study seabirds.

(　　)

TRUE OR FALSE?

本文の内容に合っていればTを、合っていなければFを書きなさい。

1) Fewer than 10% of seabirds have plastic in their stomachs.　（　　）

2) Plastic accounts for about 90% of the stomachs of seabirds.　（　　）

3) By 2050, it is expected that 99% of seabirds will have plastic in their stomachs.　（　　）

TOEIC-STYLE QUESTIONS

本文の内容に適合しているものを選びなさい。

1) How does garbage in the world's oceans affect seabirds?
   (a) The plastic in the garbage gets into the seabirds' stomachs.
   (b) It does not affect them.
   (c) It wraps around their heads.　（　　）

2) What trend has been observed?
   (a) There has been an increase in the number of birds with plastic in their stomachs.
   (b) There has been a decrease in the number of birds with plastic in their stomachs.
   (c) Things have remained basically the same.　（　　）

EXPRESSIONS

日本語の意味を表すように、本文中の単語を使って空所を埋めなさい。

1) 十代の多くがソーシャルメディアに費やす時間は現在1日に約9時間であると考えられている。

The (　　　　) (　　　　) time many teens spend on social media is now thought to be around nine hours a day.

2) 働き過ぎが健康に及ぼす影響はしばしば見過ごされる。

The (　　　　) that overwork (　　　　) on our health is often overlooked.

3) 子供のころに夢見ていた仕事に就く人は1割にも満たないということをある研究が発見した。

A study has found that (　　　　) (　　　　) one in ten people work at their childhood dream occupation.

4) アメリカでは、ガンによる死亡者の最大3割が喫煙によるものであると言われている。

In the U.S., (　　　　) (　　　　) 3 in 10 cancer deaths are said to be due to smoking.

5) 世界の人口は、2050年には100億人近くに達すると予想されている。

The world's population (　　　　) (　　　　) (　　　　) reach nearly 10 billion in the year 2050.

UNIT 11
CHINA'S LIFE-SHORTENING AIR

DEFINITIONS

次の単語の定義として最も適当なものを選びなさい。

1) shorten   (   )
2) findings (   )
3) coal   (   )
4) single   (   )
5) entire   (   )

(a) one only
(b) whole
(c) a black substance used as fuel
(d) the results of an investigation
(e) to reduce the length or duration of something

CHANGING WORDS

次の単語をカッコ内の形で答えなさい。

1) long ［動詞形］ _____
2) severe ［名詞形］ _____
3) pollution ［動詞形］ _____
4) appear ［名詞形］ _____
5) difficult ［名詞形］ _____

UNIT 11

LISTENING

英語を聞いて、カッコ内を埋めなさい。

The air in parts of China could actually (_____) your life. An international team of researchers say that severe pollution in northern China is cutting life expectancy by five (_____) a half years on average. Well, their findings appear in a study that's the first to calculate the costs of air pollution in China by using China-based (_____). Even though China's leaders have promised to rein in pollution, that, of course, will be difficult, and here's why: because China burns nearly 4 billion (_____) of coal every single year. That's nearly as much as the rest of the (_____) world put together.

NOTES

life expectancy……平均寿命
cost………………損失

WHAT'S IT ABOUT?

本文の内容をまとめているものを選びなさい。

1) China is reining in air pollution.
2) China burns less coal than the rest of the world does.
3) Severe air pollution in parts of China is decreasing life expectancy.

(   )

本文の内容に合っていればTを、合っていなければFを書きなさい。

1) Air pollution has cut life expectancy in China to 55 years. (   )
2) Reducing pollution will be difficult. (   )
3) China-based data were used in the study. (   )

本文の内容に適合しているものを選びなさい。

1) In northern China, what is the effect of air pollution on life expectancy?
   (a) It has no measurable effect.
   (b) It appears to increase life expectancy by more than five years.
   (c) It reduces life expectancy.

   (   )

2) Why will it be difficult to reduce air pollution significantly?
   (a) Because of the quantity of coal that China burns.
   (b) Because the rest of the world is uniting against China.
   (c) Because the international team of researchers is unlikely to cooperate.

   (   )

UNIT 11

日本語の意味を表すように、本文中の単語を使って空所を埋めなさい。

1) 定期的な運動は、心臓病のリスクを大幅に減らすことができる。

   Regular physical activity can decrease the risk of heart disease
   (   ) a considerable amount.

2) 日本で生まれた赤ん坊は、平均で83歳以上まで生きると期待されている。

   Babies born in Japan today can be expected (   )
   (   ) to live to more than 83 years of age.

3) 宇宙飛行士ユーリ・ガガーリンは、大気圏外に旅をした最初の人だ。

   The astronaut Yuri Gagarin was (   ) (   )
   (   ) journey into outer space.

4) 死に直面していたけれど、消防士は子供たちを救出するために家の中に入った。

   (   ) (   ) he faced nearly certain death, the
   firefighter went into the house to rescue the children.

5) 医療専門家は抗生物質の無責任な使用を抑制しようとしている。

   Medical professionals are trying to (   ) (   )
   irresponsible use of antibiotics.

UNIT 12
PROSTHETIC LIMBS FROM 3-D PRINTERS

DEFINITIONS

次の単語の定義として最も適当なものを選びなさい。

1) violence   (   )
2) victim   (   )
3) plight   (   )
4) magazine   (   )
5) amputee   (   )

(a) someone whose leg or arm has been removed
(b) someone who has been harmed as a result of an accident or crime
(c) the use of physical force in order to injure
(d) a sad or difficult situation
(e) a kind of book with a thin cover, usually published once a week or month

CHANGING WORDS

次の単語をカッコ内の形で答えなさい。

1) innocent [名詞形] _____
2) lost [原形] _____
3) explosion [動詞形] _____
4) fly [過去分詞形] _____
5) use [名詞形] _____

UNIT 12

LISTENING

英語を聞いて、カッコ内を埋めなさい。

The violence in South Sudan has (_____) in an appalling number of innocent victims who've (_____) wounded, crippled or disfigured. In 2012, 14-year old Daniel Omar lost both arms in a (_____) explosion. His plight, described in a *Time* magazine story, (_____) a Los Angeles man to fly to South Sudan to give the boy prosthetic arms. Now, many amputee children are getting prosthetic (_____) using revolutionary 3-D printer technology.

NOTES

appalling ……… 恐るべき
cripple ………… [手足を] 不自由にする
Time …………『タイム』(1923年に創刊されたアメリカの週間ニュース誌)
magazine ……… 雑誌
revolutionary ‥ 画期的な
wound ………… 〜を傷つける
disfigure ……… 〜を傷つける
prosthetic …… 人工装具の
3-D (three-dimensional) … 3次元の

WHAT'S IT ABOUT?

本文の内容をまとめているものを選びなさい。

1) Daniel Omar has had a very difficult life.
2) Thanks to 3-D printing, many amputees can now get artificial limbs.
3) *Time* magazine has launched a campaign to reduce the number of bombs in South Sudan.

(　　)

本文の内容に合っていればTを、合っていなければFを書きなさい。

1) Many people have been injured in the violence in South Sudan.　　　　　　　　　　　　　　　　　　　　(　　)
2) Daniel Omar lost both legs.　　　　　　　(　　)
3) A man in Los Angeles flew to South Sudan to give Daniel Omar prosthetic arms.　　　　　　　　　　　　(　　)

TOEIC-STYLE QUESTIONS

本文の内容に適合しているものを選びなさい。

1) When did Daniel Omar lose both his arms?
   (a) In 2012.
   (b) In 2014.
   (c) Last year.　　　　　　　　　　　　　(　　)

2) What technology is helping people to replace their amputated limbs?
   (a) Revolving doors.
   (b) Explosives.
   (c) 3-D printing.　　　　　　　　　　　　(　　)

UNIT 12

EXPRESSIONS

日本語の意味を表すように、本文中の単語を使って空所を埋めなさい。

1) 業績不振はその会社のリーダーの交代を生じさせた。
   The poor business performance (　　　　)(　　　　) a change of leadership at the company.

2) 自国のための戦闘中に負傷した兵士は、政府によって十分にケアを受けるべきだ。
   Soldiers (　　　　) while fighting for their country should be adequately cared for by the government.

3) その物語は、祖母が私に話してくれたが、感激のあまりに背筋がゾクゾクした。
   The story, (　　　　) to me by my grandmother, sent chills up my spine.

4) 海外からの留学生の自信に満ちて流ちょうな英語はもっと一生懸命に勉強する動機付けとなった。
   The confidence and fluent English of the overseas students (　　　　) me (　　　　) study harder.

5) 燃料として石炭を使う発電所は、汚染と気象変動の主な原因だ。
   Power stations (　　　　) coal as fuel are a major source of pollution and climate change.

UNIT 13
NZ MAKES CYBERBULLYING ILLEGAL

DEFINITIONS

次の単語の定義として最も適当なものを選びなさい。

1) bully　　　(　　)
2) bill　　　　(　　)
3) incite　　　(　　)
4) offender　(　　)
5) remove　　(　　)

(a) a document with a proposal for a new law
(b) to encourage people to do something bad
(c) to frighten or hurt someone weaker than you
(d) a person who commits a crime
(e) to take away

CHANGING WORDS

次の単語をカッコ内の形で答えなさい。

1) illegal [反意語] _____
2) communication [動詞形] _____
3) mean [過去分詞形] _____
4) approve [名詞形] _____
5) remove [名詞形] _____

UNIT 13

LISTENING

英語を聞いて、カッコ内を埋めなさい。

Now, let's (_____) to New Zealand. The nation has just made cyberbullying illegal. The new Harmful Digital Communications Bill (_____) anyone who sends threatening, harmful or racist messages can be fined or jailed. If the harmful messages are (_____) enough—for example, inciting (_____)—the offender can be jailed for up to three years. Also, companies like Facebook and Twitter now have to work with an approved agency to remove offensive (_____).

NOTES

Harmful Digital Communications Bill ……… 有害デジタル通信法案
threatening ……脅迫的な   racist ……… 人種差別主義（者）の
jail ………………〜を投獄する   offensive ……不快感を与える
post ……………投稿

WHAT'S IT ABOUT?

本文の内容をまとめているものを選びなさい。

1) New Zealand is working to reduce the economic power of Facebook and Twitter.
2) New Zealand has increased the number of crimes for which three-year sentences apply.
3) Cyberbullying has been made illegal in New Zealand.

(   )

本文の内容に合っていればTを、合っていなければFを書きなさい。

1) Cyberbullying is illegal in New Zealand. ( )

2) In New Zealand, people sending threatening messages can be fined. ( )

3) All commercial Facebook content has to be approved by an agency before posting. ( )

TOEIC-STYLE QUESTIONS

本文の内容に適合しているものを選びなさい。

1) Which of the following is true about the Harmful Digital Communications Bill?
    (a) It allows for penalties of more than three years.
    (b) It has become law in New Zealand.
    (c) It is illegal to use Twitter. ( )

2) Which of the following is cyberbullying?
    (a) Sending too many messages.
    (b) Sending a threatening message.
    (c) Failing to get approval from an agency. ( )

UNIT 13

日本語の意味を表すように、本文中の単語を使って空所を埋めなさい。

1) 試験中に他の学生に話しかける者は誰でも失格になる。

   (　　　　) (　　　　　) speaks to another student during the exam will be disqualified.

2) 車を駐車するとき、彼は標識を見逃して、後で駐車違反で罰金を科された。

   When parking his car, he failed to notice the signs and (　　　　) later (　　　　) for a parking violation.

3) 多くの国で、政治に関する抗議運動に参加している人は投獄される危険にさらされる。

   In many countries, people taking part in political protests risk (　　　　) (　　　　).

4) アマゾンやグーグルのような一流企業で仕事を得ることは技術的あるいは管理経営の手腕と熱心さを必要とする。

   Getting a job at a top company (　　　　) Amazon or Google requires technical or administrative skills and dedication.

5) イギリスでは医療サービスへの高まる需要のため、患者が予約のために最大で1年待たなければならないというときがある。

   Growing demand for medical services in the UK means that patients sometimes (　　　　) (　　　　) wait for up to a year for an appointment.

UNIT 14
MUSICAL TASTE AND PERSONALITY

次の単語の定義として最も適当なものを選びなさい。

1) trait　　　　　　(　　)
2) indie　　　　　　(　　)
3) introverted　　　(　　)
4) intelligent　　　(　　)
5) self-confidence (　　)

(a) a feature of one's personality
(b) a feeling that one can do things well
(c) good at learning and able to understand difficult things
(d) quiet and preferring to spend time alone
(e) made by a small company

CHANGING WORDS

次の単語をカッコ内の形で答えなさい。

1) music [形容詞形] ＿＿＿＿＿＿＿＿＿＿＿＿＿＿＿＿＿＿＿
2) honest [名詞形] ＿＿＿＿＿＿＿＿＿＿＿＿＿＿＿＿＿＿＿
3) introverted [反意語] ＿＿＿＿＿＿＿＿＿＿＿＿＿＿＿＿＿
4) classical [名詞形] ＿＿＿＿＿＿＿＿＿＿＿＿＿＿＿＿＿
5) intelligent [名詞形] ＿＿＿＿＿＿＿＿＿＿＿＿＿＿＿＿

UNIT 14

LISTENING

英語を聞いて、カッコ内を埋めなさい。

A university in Edinburgh (＿＿＿＿＿) 36,000 people about their favorite music and (＿＿＿＿＿) traits. They found that fans of pop artists—like Beyonce, maybe Taylor Swift—were often honest people but lacked creativity. Fans of indie (＿＿＿＿＿), such as Radiohead, (＿＿＿＿＿) often introverted and not very hardworking. And those who listened to classical music, such as Beethoven, were found to be highly intelligent and brimming with self-(＿＿＿＿＿).

NOTES

Edinburgh	エジンバラ（スコットランドの首都）
Beyonce	ビヨンセ（米国のシンガーソングライター、ダンサー、音楽プロデューサー、女優）
Taylor Swift	テイラー・スウィフト（米国のカントリーポップ歌手、シンガーソングライター、女優）
Radiohead	レディオヘッド（英国のロックバンド）
Beethoven	ベートーヴェン（ドイツの作曲家、バッハ等と並んで音楽史上極めて重要な作曲家で、日本では「楽聖」と呼ばれる

WHAT'S IT ABOUT?

本文の内容をまとめているものを選びなさい。

1) A Scottish university is stepping up its research into the population's preferences.

2) People's tastes in music appear to be a predictor of their personality.

3) Beyonce and Taylor Swift are not very creative.

(　　)

本文の内容に合っていればTを、合っていなければFを書きなさい。

1) Fans of popular music appear to be dishonest. 　　　(　　)
2) Fans of indie bands were found to be introverted. 　　(　　)
3) Radiohead is an indie band. 　　　　　　　　　　　(　　)

TOEIC-STYLE QUESTIONS

本文の内容に適合しているものを選びなさい。

1) Fans of which kind of music were found to lack creativity?
   (a) Pop music.
   (b) Indie music.
   (c) Classical music. 　　　　　　　　　　　　　　　(　　)

2) What was found about classical music listeners?
   (a) They lack confidence.
   (b) They are very hardworking.
   (c) They are intelligent. 　　　　　　　　　　　　　(　　)

UNIT 14

日本語の意味を表すように、本文中の単語を使って空所を埋めなさい。

1) 会社のために人を雇うときには、誠実さの無い人を避けるように気を付けなさい。
   When hiring people for your company, be sure to avoid people who (　　　　) integrity.

2) レモンやオレンジやグレープフルーツのような柑橘系の果物は、ビタミンCの良い供給源だ。
   Citrus fruits (　　　　)(　　　　) lemons, oranges, and grapefruit are good sources of Vitamin C.

3) 良いことは待っている人たちにやってくる。
   Good things come to (　　　　)(　　　　) wait.

4) 1983年に、HIVはAIDSを引き起こすウイルスであると発見された。
   In 1983, HIV was (　　　　)(　　　　)(　　　　) the virus that causes AIDS.

5) ライブが始まるのを待っているときに、聴衆は期待でいっぱいになっていた。
   The audience were (　　　　)(　　　　) anticipation as they waited for the gig to start.

MORNING-PERSON GENES

DEFINITIONS

次の単語の定義として最も適当なものを選びなさい。

1) curse （　　）
2) alarm （　　）
3) lazy （　　）
4) insomnia （　　）
5) depression （　　）

(a) not willing to do work
(b) difficulty getting to sleep
(c) a state of extreme unhappiness
(d) a thing we use to wake us up
(e) to blame angrily, often using bad language

CHANGING WORDS

次の単語をカッコ内の形で答えなさい。

1) hit [過去分詞形] _____
2) genetic [名詞形] _____
3) suggest [名詞形] _____
4) associate [名詞形] _____
5) less [原級] _____

英語を聞いて、カッコ内を埋めなさい。

Well, do you curse the alarm when it goes off in the morning, (_____) hit the snooze button five, 10 times before getting up? Well, don't (_____)—you're not lazy. It makes me feel good, this new research we're about to tell you. See, it suggests that (_____) a morning person or not is genetic. It (_____) 15 genetic variants associated with what it called "morningness," and that morning people are less likely to suffer from insomnia or depression. So you can blame that snoozing on your (_____).

NOTES

go off ············· 突然鳴り出す
snooze button ··· スヌーズボタン（目覚まし時計のアラームを一旦止めて、短時間後にまた鳴るようにするボタン）
variant ············· 変異
snooze ············· うたた寝する、居眠りする

本文の内容をまとめているものを選びなさい。

1) Alarm clocks should be designed better.
2) Whether or not a person finds it easy to get up in the morning may have a genetic reason.
3) Using a snooze button too often may cause depression.

(　　)

TRUE OR FALSE?

本文の内容に合っていればTを、合っていなければFを書きなさい。

1) Hitting the snooze button in the morning is not necessarily a sign of laziness. (　　)

2) Morning people are less likely to suffer from insomnia. (　　)

3) Scientists have no idea why some people find it easier than others to get up. (　　)

TOEIC-STYLE QUESTIONS

本文の内容に適合しているものを選びなさい。

1) What is "morningness"?
   (a) A newly discovered gene.
   (b) The tendency to avoid mornings.
   (c) The tendency to like mornings. (　　)

2) Which of the following is NOT true?
   (a) A survey has found that on average people hit the snooze button eight times every morning.
   (b) Genetic variants may be connected to our sleeping and waking patterns.
   (c) A snooze button is a device for turning off the alarm temporarily. (　　)

UNIT 15

日本語の意味を表すように、本文中の単語を使って空所を埋めなさい。

1) 自分の失敗をすぐに他の人のせいにするべきではない。

   You shouldn't immediately (　　　　) your failures (　　　　) other people.

2) 運動不足と過食は糖尿病と関係がある。

   A lack of exercise and overeating are (　　　　) (　　　　) diabetes.

3) 裕福な人は他人に注意を払う可能性が低いということを最近の研究が示唆している。

   Recent studies have suggested that rich people are (　　　　) (　　　　) (　　　　) pay attention to other people.

4) 電話が鳴ったときに私はちょうど学校に出かけようとしていた。

   I was just (　　　　) (　　　　) leave for school when the phone rang.

5) 偶然に暴発する銃は、損傷あるいは死さえ引き起こす可能性があるので、所有者はそれらの弾を抜いておくようにアドバイスされている。

   A gun (　　　　) (　　　　) accidentally can cause injuries or even death, so owners are advised to keep them unloaded.

CNNショートニュースで学ぶ総合英語

©2019年1月31日 初版発行

検印
省略

編著者 　　　　　　　安 浪 誠 祐
　　　　　　　　　　Richard S. Lavin

発行者 　　　　　　　原　雅 久
発行所 　　　　　　株式会社 朝日出版社
　　　　　〒101-0065 東京都千代田区西神田 3-3-5
　　　　　　　　電話　東京 (03) 3239-0271
　　　　　　　　FAX　東京 (03) 3239-0479
　　　　　　　　E-mail: text-e@asahipress.com
　　　　　　　　振替口座　00140-2-46008
　　　　　　　　http://www.asahipress.com/
　　　　　　組版・メディアアート／製版・錦明印刷

乱丁・落丁本はお取り替えいたします。
ISBN 978-4-255-15643-9

時代の最先端を伝えるCNNで最新の英語をキャッチ！

ちょっと手ごわい でも効果絶大！

世界の重大事件から日常のおもしろネタ、スターや著名人のインタビューなど、CNNの多彩なニュースを生の音声とともにお届けします。さらに、充実した内容の特集や連載によって、実践的な英語力が身につきます。

表紙イメージは2018年11月号

英語力が伸びる！4つのポイント

❶ **目的別学習ガイドの充実！**
「EEを買ったはいいけど、いまいち使い方がわからない」─もうそんな心配はいりません。EEでは、目的に合わせた学習モデルを提示。自分にぴったりの学習方法がきっと見つかるはず！

❷ **本気で英語力をつけるための「繰り返し学習」**
「忙しいから、とりあえず聞き流すだけ…」では、本当の実力は身につきません。厳選された素材を「精聴」し、何度も聴く「繰り返し学習」によって、初めて英語力がつき、聞き取りが可能になります。「精聴」、しかる後に「多聴」が、学習の王道です。

❸ **継続学習を実現する最適な学習量**
「精聴」による学習効果を最大限に得るために分量を最適化。気に入った素材を繰り返し聴くことで、リスニング力、発信力をはじめとする英語力が確実に向上し、さらに継続的な学習が可能になります。

❹ **2020年東京五輪を見据えた、充実の新連載！**
NHK英語元講師・江口裕之先生の「英語で伝えるニッポン」や、マンガとゲームで日本を学んだベンジャミン・ボアズ氏のエッセイを絶賛連載中。

iPhone、iPad で読める電子版もApp Store で大好評発売中！

CNN ENGLISH EXPRESS
CNNライブ収録CD付き
毎月6日発売
定価1,240円（税込）
http://ee.asahipress.com/

朝日出版社 〒101-0065 東京都千代田区西神田 3-3-5 TEL 03-3263-3321

生きた英語でリスニング！

CNN ニュース・リスニング

1本30秒だから、聞きやすい！

2018［秋冬］　生声CD・対訳付き・A5判　本体1000円＋税

世界標準の英語ニュースがだれでも
聞き取れるようになる［30秒×3回聞き］方式！

- 大坂なおみ、全米オープン優勝の快挙！
- 「ゲーム障害」をWHOが病気と認定
- レディー・ガガ、反性暴力の声を上げる…など

スティーブ・ジョブズ 伝説のスピーチ＆プレゼン

- 伝説のスタンフォード大学スピーチ
- 驚異のプレゼンでたどるジョブズの軌跡
- 伝記本の著者が明かすカリスマの素顔
- CNNが振り返るジョブズの功績

生声CD・対訳付き・A5判　本体1000円＋税

スタンフォードの「英語ができる自分」になる教室

ケリー・マクゴニガル　生声CD・対訳付き・A5判　本体1000円＋税

意識が変われば英語力はぐんぐん伸びる！英語をモノにする意志力の鍛え方、
「なりたい自分」になるための戦略…など、だれも教えてくれなかった「学習のひみつ」を
スタンフォード大学人気講師が解き明かす。

セレブたちの卒業式スピーチ

次世代に贈る言葉　生声CD・対訳付き・A5判　本体1200円＋税

アメリカ名門大学で語られた未来を担う者たちへのメッセージ

- ビル＆メリンダ・ゲイツ
- メリル・ストリープ［女優］
- ティム・クック［アップルCEO］
- アーノルド・シュワルツェネッガー
- イーロン・マスク［テスラモーターズCEO］

朝日出版社　〒101-0065 東京都千代田区西神田 3-3-5　TEL 03-3263-3321

最高クオリティの問題と解説により
圧倒的な効率でスコアUP！

韓国TOEIC運営企業YBM社が30年間のノウハウで頻出形式を徹底的に分析！

YBM TOEIC 研究所＝著　各本体3,400円+税　B5判変型

韓国TOEIC運営企業の究極の模試×10回分

TOEIC® L&Rテスト YBM超実戦模試 リスニング1000問

TOEIC® L&Rテスト YBM超実戦模試 リーディング1000問

リスニング
460ページ（本冊168頁、別冊292頁）

MP3音声CD-ROM＋3パターンの音声ダウンロード付き

▶付属CD-ROMに通常音声を収録。
▶ダウンロードでは通常音声のほか
〈1.2倍速音声〉
〈本番環境に近い雑音入り音声〉
も提供。

リーディング
528ページ（本冊336頁、別冊192頁）

朝日出版社　〒101-0065 東京都千代田区西神田 3-3-5　TEL 03-3263-3321